COCAINE

BY ALEXIS BURLING

CONTENT CONSULTANT
MEAGHAN C. CREED, PHD
ASSISTANT PROFESSOR OF PHARMACOLOGY
UNIVERSITY OF MARYLAND, SCHOOL OF MEDICINE

Essential Library

An Imprint of Abdo Publishing | abdopublishing.com

Published by Abdo Publishing, a division of ABDO, PO Box 398166, Minneapolis, Minnesota 55439.
Copyright © 2019 by Abdo Consulting Group, Inc. International copyrights reserved in all countries.
No part of this book may be reproduced in any form without written permission from the publisher.
Essential Library™ is a trademark and logo of Abdo Publishing.

Printed in the United States of America, North Mankato, Minnesota
042018
092018

Cover Photo: Shutterstock Images
Interior Photos: Chris Pizzello/Invision/AP Images, 4–5; Jackson Lee/starmaxinc.com/AP Images,
9; Shutterstock Images, 12–13, 21, 31, 53; Wesley Bocxe/Science Source, 17; US Drug Enforcement
Agency, 22; Mark Lennihan/AP Images, 25; Alec Macdonald/Alamy, 27; Raul Arboleda/AFP/Getty
Images, 29; Authenticated News/Archive Photos/Getty Images, 34–35; Rodrigo Abd/AP Images, 37;
Smith Collection/Gado/Archive Photos/Getty Images, 39; Fernando Vergara/AP Images, 41, 43; Red
Line Editorial, 44–45; AP Images, 49; Callista Images/Cultura/Glow Images, 54; Fernando Da Cunha/
Science Source, 59; Brookhaven National Laboratory/Science Source, 58; Diego Cervo/iStockphoto,
61; Lawrence Migdale/Science Source, 62; Monkey Business Images/Shutterstock Images, 65; Oscar
Burriel/Science Source, 68; Josh Thompson/Cal Sport Media/AP Images, 74; iStockphoto, 76–77,
88–89; Mika/Corbis/Glow, 80–81; Juan Monino/iStockphoto, 83; Photononstop/Superstock, 84;
Deposit Photos/Glow Images, 93, 96; Milica Stankovic/iStockphoto, 95; Monkey Business Images/
iStockphoto, 99

Editor: Kate Conley
Series Designer: Laura Polzin

Library of Congress Control Number: 2017961350

Publisher's Cataloging-in-Publication Data

Names: Burling, Alexis, author.
Title: Cocaine / by Alexis Burling.
Description: Minneapolis, Minnesota : Abdo Publishing, 2019. | Series: Drugs in real life | Includes
        online resources and index.
Identifiers: ISBN 9781532114144 (lib.bdg.) | ISBN 9781532153976 (ebook)
Subjects: LCSH: Cocaine--Juvenile literature. | Cocaine abuse--Juvenile literature. | Recreational
        drug use--Juvenile literature. | Drug control--United States--Juvenile literature.
Classification: DDC 362.299--dc23

CHAPTER ONE

A BATTLE WITH COCAINE ADDICTION

In the opening frame of her 2017 tell-all documentary, *Simply Complicated*, singer and actress Demi Lovato doesn't come off like a mega-famous celebrity. Plopped down on a couch and wearing blue jeans and a striped button-down shirt, the 25-year-old star could pass as the girl next door. But when asked why she feels nervous about being interviewed for the film, Lovato reveals something not even close to normal: "Because the last time I did an interview this long, I was on cocaine."[1]

Demi Lovato's documentary *Simply Complicated* revealed her struggles with drug addiction.

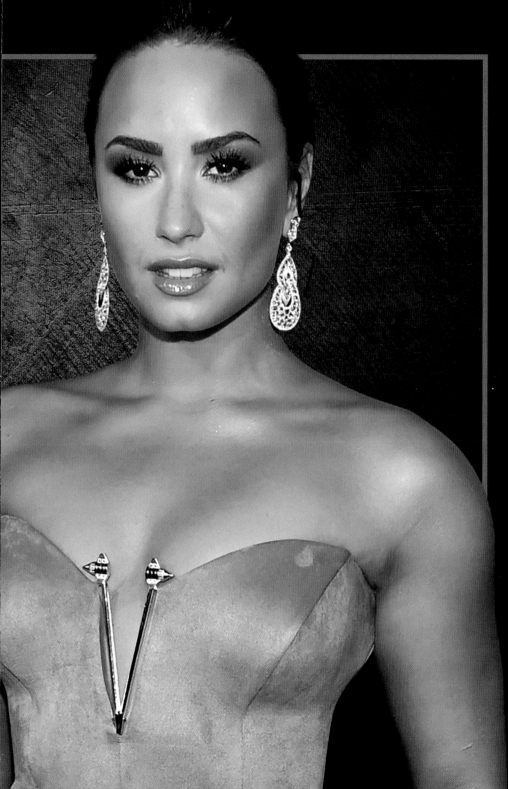

Lovato's struggles with drugs are no secret. Since the former Disney Channel star rocketed to fame in 2009 at the age of 17, she has been open about her love of partying and feeling out of control. In just a few short years, Lovato experienced extraordinary high points in her career. She also went through devastating, debilitating lows. In her 2013 memoir, *Staying Strong: 365 Days a Year*, she shared one dark confession after another about battling an eating disorder, a cutting habit, and her complicated relationship with cocaine.

"[It's] something I've never talked about before, but with my drug use I could hide it to where I would sneak drugs. I couldn't go 30 minutes to an hour without cocaine, and I would bring it on airplanes," Lovato told *Access Hollywood*. "I would smuggle it basically and just wait until everyone in first class would go to sleep, and I would do it right there. I'd sneak to the bathroom and I'd do it."[2]

HEREDITARY HABITS

No one is an exact replica of his or her parents. But most people inherit genetic traits or behavioral patterns from their mother, father, and grandparents. Some health experts say traits associated with addiction, such as impulsive behavior and an inability to deal with stress in a healthy manner, are often passed down from generation to generation. That may have played a role in Lovato's life. Her father abused both alcohol and addictive drugs. Lovato attributes her early curiosity about cocaine in small part to his behavior. As she said in *Simply Complicated,* "I guess I always searched for what (my dad) found in drugs and alcohol because it fulfilled him, and he chose that over a family."[3]

EARLY FAME

Demi Lovato was born on August 20, 1992, in Albuquerque, New Mexico. As a child, Lovato loved to sing and dance and started performing professionally at an early age. She entered beauty pageants with her older sister and took voice lessons. In 2002, when she turned ten, Lovato got her first big break. She landed a regular role on the children's television show *Barney & Friends*. From there, she guest starred on a number of other TV shows and released a debut album, *Don't Forget*. In 2009, she even got her own Disney Channel show, *Sonny with a Chance*.

During that whirlwind time, Lovato's life wasn't all signing autographs, chatting with fans, and having fun on the set. As she reveals in *Simply Complicated*, her life was drastically changing—almost too drastically. She faced mounting pressure to succeed and felt she needed something to take the edge off. Lovato and her friend Marissa Callahan began staying out late and drinking—a lot.

PRESSURE TO PARTY

Peer pressure can play a big role in drug use. Some people try illegal substances to fit in. They like the way the drug makes them feel, so they keep doing it. Many start with something easily accessible, like alcohol. Then they graduate to harder drugs, like cocaine. That's what happened to Lovato.

"We started drinking fairly early," said Marissa Callahan, Lovato's close friend in high school. "To me, it was like, 'We're just having fun. We're kids. Everyone's doing it, so we're going to, too.' Little did we know that there was going to be, like, this downward spiral."[4]

When Demi was 17, she decided to stretch her boundaries even further. She tried cocaine. "I was scared because my mom always told me that your heart could just burst if you do it," Lovato says. "But I did it anyways, and I loved it."[5]

SWIFT ADDICTION

Lovato's experimentation with drugs soon turned into an obsession. She began to count on the high in order to get through the day. While Lovato was touring with the Jonas Brothers in 2009, her behavior became erratic. According to her manager, Phil McIntyre, Demi alternated between being depressed and sleeping all the time to being extraordinarily aggressive. In one particular headline-grabbing incident,

Adderall is a highly addictive and often abused stimulant. Doctors prescribe it to increase attention span and focus, control behavioral problems, and tone down hyperactivity.

Lovato punched one of her backup dancers in the face for going public about Lovato's dependency on the prescription drug Adderall. To make matters worse, Lovato also could not get control of her cocaine habit. "I just came to a breaking point," Lovato says.[6]

Feeling guilty about the punching episode and desperate to get her life back under control, Lovato abandoned the tour and entered a drug rehabilitation center. There, she was diagnosed

with bipolar disorder, an illness of the brain that causes drastic shifts in mood and energy levels and interferes with a person's ability to carry out everyday tasks. Doctors watched her around the clock. But even with the diagnosis and proper treatment, Lovato still wasn't ready to leave behind her drug-doing ways after she was discharged.

Lovato was high during interviews in which she talked about her supposed sobriety. She carried cocaine in her purse while on the job and faked drug tests by using other people's urine. She even tried to commit suicide by mixing cocaine with a near-lethal dosage of Xanax and other prescription pills and ended up in a psychiatric hospital. "I wasn't working my program. I wasn't ready to get sober. I was sneaking [coke] on planes, sneaking it in bathrooms, sneaking it throughout the night. Nobody knew," Lovato says. "I went on like a bender of like two months where I was using daily."[7]

Finally, when Lovato was 19, her family, life coach, and business manager staged an intervention. They made her give up her phone so she couldn't contact drug dealers. She also had to move into a halfway house, a place where people with addictions can practice the lessons they learned in rehab. Lovato lived there for about a year. She had to do chores, participate in group meetings, be home before curfew, and abide by strictly enforced rules. Neither she nor any of her roommates were allowed to do drugs or drink alcohol at any time, either on or off the premises.

Luckily, the time spent at the halfway house helped. Soon Lovato felt strong enough to move into her own house and adopt a few dogs. Best of all, by 2017, she had successfully transitioned into a drug-free lifestyle.

The ending to Demi Lovato's story is a positive one—at least for now. But for Lovato and other people who use drugs, staying sober is an ongoing challenge. According to the National Institute on Drug Abuse, the tendency for relapse, or falling back into drug use, is the highest between one and six months into abstinence.

INTERVENTIONS

People with drug addictions damage their own brains and bodies. But they also inflict harm on their loved ones, who lose hope every time they fail to get clean. Some families give up entirely. Others stage interventions. The interventions can take the form of simple heart-to-heart talks with those closest to the person with the drug problem. In more serious situations, a psychiatrist, licensed drug counselor, or other doctor will get involved. The doctors explain treatment options and present a plan for what to do if the treatment doesn't work. It is a grueling and uncomfortable process. But interventions can help save lives.

THE DANGERS OF COCAINE

Cocaine, sometimes called coke for short, is one of the hardest drugs to quit. It is a highly addictive substance that comes from the coca plant, which is native to South America. The leaves are processed and turned into a white powder that can be snorted

Cocaine is an alkaloid, a type of chemical compound containing nitrogen that is found in plants. Other alkaloids include nicotine and morphine.

or injected. It can also be smoked after being turned into a crystalized form, crack cocaine.

Once in the bloodstream, cocaine travels to the brain, where it causes long-term changes in the function of brain cells. Users

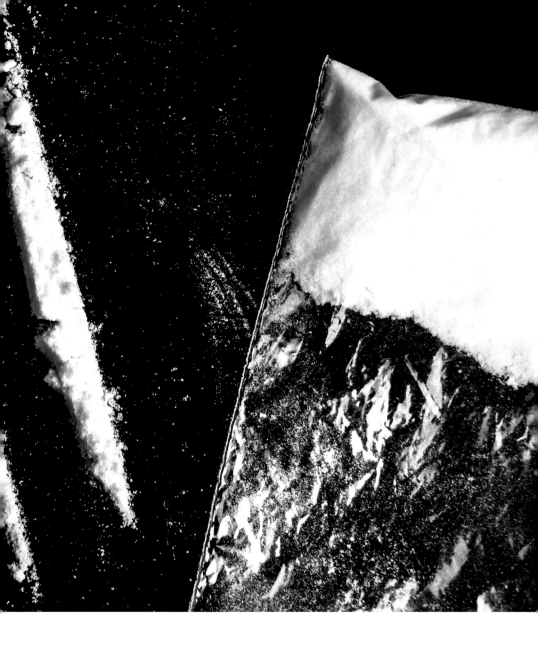

report feeling euphoric after the first sniff. But the problem with coke—and with most addictive substances—is that the high wears off quickly. Users need to do more in order to feel good and capture the same feeling as the initial high. Negative

WHAT'S IN THIS COKE?

Many drug manufacturers and dealers mix, or cut, cocaine with other substances to bulk up their stash before it is sold. Expecting the coke to be pure, unsuspecting buyers are often surprised by the differences in high from one bag to another. Aside from things like sugar and talcum powder, some of the most common additives used in cocaine include:

- Ground-up glass
- Benzocaine, a skin-numbing agent used in suntan lotions and first aid creams
- Boric acid, a substance used as an insecticide or flame retardant
- Dimethyl terephthalate, a substance used to make rodent poison or plastic
- Lidocaine, a skin-numbing agent or a treatment for irregular heartbeats
- Levamisole, a medication used to treat worm infections in the body— mostly in cattle
- Hydroxyzine, an antihistamine used to relieve itching, hives, and other skin rashes

mood swings develop when the drug isn't taken consistently. Long-time users take more and more just to feel normal.

Cocaine affects more than just the brain. It also permanently impairs the rest of the body's ability to function. Among other consequences, it causes shortness of breath and can cause cardiac arrest in certain users, even on the first try.

Cocaine is illegal in the United States and using it, possessing it, or selling it can land a person in jail. Even if one avoids criminal action, cocaine is an expensive habit. At the high end, one pure gram costs about $150 in the United States.[8] There are cheaper options available on the street. But sometimes those are mixed with other harmful substances, such as rat poison or even other drugs, such as amphetamine. These often have devastating side effects.

For people who are currently battling cocaine addiction or know someone who just can't figure out how to stop, there are plenty of resources that might help. Free national hotlines provide guidance at all hours of the day and night. Rehab centers have experienced physicians and nurses who create and help implement treatment plans. Nonprofit groups, houses of worship, and other socially minded community organizations provide ongoing online or in-person support for those in need.

Cocaine users usually consume the drug in binges. They snort or inject the drug repeatedly within a short period of time, at increasingly higher doses, to maintain their high.

Drug use is a worldwide epidemic. Cocaine is a particularly powerful drug that is widely used around the world. But with dedicated attention and support, the problem is not insurmountable. Staying informed is the first step.

CHAPTER TWO

WHAT IS COCAINE?

While Demi Lovato and other celebrities with addictions receive a lot of high-profile media attention, the problem extends far beyond Hollywood. Cocaine addiction affects all parts of society, regardless of age, race, gender, or income level. Each year more than 1.5 million people experience cocaine addiction. In 2016, more than 500,000 of those adults age 18 or older sought treatment.[1] So what is cocaine—and why is it so easy to get hooked on it?

Cocaine is a stimulant drug found in the leaves of *Erythoxylum coca*, a shrub-like plant that grows in parts of South America. The plant's leaves are dried and processed. Then the

A cultivated coca plant grows three to four feet (1 to 1.3 m) tall, and farmers harvest its elliptical-shaped leaves up to four times per year.

drug is extracted and transformed into a white powder, which is known as cocaine. In many cases, the cocaine is then combined with other white, powdery substances such as baby powder, flour, cornstarch, baking soda, or sugar. These fillers increase the profit margins for drug dealers. Other times, the cocaine is mixed with ground-up amphetamines, speed, or even rat poison. These fillers can result in a sharper, speedier, more dangerous high.

After the cocaine is prepped, the powder is separated into plastic bags of various sizes. It is sold to drug dealers by weight in grams. Interested individuals can then buy cocaine on the street in any quantity they choose. Depending on how pure the powder is and where the customer is purchasing the drug, the price of a gram of cocaine can vary widely. A 2015 study found prices ranging from approximately $10 in Brazil to a whopping $235 in Australia.[2]

Cocaine has many street names, including coke, rock, snow, blow, candy, Charlie, C, bump, flake, powder, and toot.

HOW IS COCAINE USED?

In many cases, cocaine is one of the most expensive illegal drugs to buy, especially in large quantities. Despite the cost, it's also one of the most popular. According to the National Institute on Drug Abuse, cocaine is one of the most commonly abused illegal drugs in the United States after marijuana and prescription drugs.

Cocaine is a stimulant, a category of drug that affects the nervous system. Similar to the feeling people would get after drinking three or four cups of strong coffee in the morning, doing cocaine boosts energy levels and mental awareness. The drug helps users feel more confident and in control of day-to-day tasks. But there's also a downside. A cocaine high always triggers a crash—a period of depression and often intense anxiety. Users need increasingly higher doses to pick themselves up after a crash and maintain the same level of high.

Most cocaine users snort the drug through their nose. First, they pour the white powder onto a hard surface, often a mirror or a glass table. Then, they cut it into a series of lines using a sharp tool, such as a razor blade or credit card. When everything is ready, they inhale a small amount, called a bump, one line at a time, using a straw or a

THE 8 BALL

Unlike most things in the United States, quantities of cocaine are measured using the metric system. That means the drug is bought and sold in grams, not ounces. One of the most common amounts to buy is 3.5 grams, often called an 8 ball. The name *8 ball* comes from the fact that 3.5 grams is about one-eighth of an ounce.

In the United States, a 2017 study done by *Narcotic News* found that an 8 ball can cost anywhere from approximately $75 in Tucson, Arizona, to about $350 in Honolulu, Hawaii.[3] Sometimes, if the product is less pure or the dealer is trying to unload his or her stash, the price of an 8 ball can drop even lower. Buyers interested in less than an 8 ball can get what's called a teener. Short for *teenager*, a teener is half the size of an 8 ball.

rolled up banknote. Some people rub what's left on their lips and gums for a numbing effect. From nose to brain, the process of getting high takes less than 5 minutes and lasts between 15 and 30 minutes.[4]

Other cocaine users prefer a quicker high. They dissolve the powder in water and inject the milky substance into the bloodstream using a hypodermic syringe and needle. It takes a much shorter time for the liquid to travel to the brain. The initial high happens in less than 15 seconds and lasts for 5 to 10 minutes, depending on the dosage.[5]

WHAT IS CRACK?

A third, even riskier method of getting high on cocaine also exists. It's the most addictive and the most dangerous form of cocaine—crack. Crack is a type of cocaine that looks like a bunch of crystals. It is formed when cocaine, water, and sodium bicarbonate (baking soda) are combined, then heated. As the mixture boils, solids are

WHAT IS FREEBASE COCAINE?

Freebase cocaine is the solid form, or base, of cocaine. Manufacturers take the white powder and combine it with water and ammonia. Then, they take a highly volatile and flammable liquid called diethyl ether and use it to separate the cocaine base from the solution. The end result is a form of cocaine that is nearly 100 percent pure. As with crack, users do the drug by smoking and inhaling it. The high lasts for about 30 minutes.[6] Not only is freebase cocaine dangerous to use, it can also be dangerous to produce. Many drug labs have exploded in the process.

separated from the liquid, cooled, and dried. Then they are broken into tiny chunks, often referred to as rocks.

Much like the process of smoking marijuana, crack crystals are placed at the end of a glass tube or pipe. The rocks are heated, and the vapor is inhaled. The resulting high happens

Snorting cocaine not only damages the brain and nervous system but also can cause nose bleeds, loss of smell, and nasal disfigurement.

almost immediately after smoking and lasts for up to 10 minutes.[7]

Because crack is inhaled directly into the lungs as a smoke, it reaches the brain more quickly than powdered cocaine that is inhaled through the nose.

Some studies suggest the swiftness of delivery boosts crack's addictive qualities. Because the high doesn't last as long, users need to inhale more over a shorter period of time to maintain the high. This means crack smokers are at a greater risk of doing too much crack in one session. Serious consequences include increased toxin levels in the blood, shortness of breath, and aggressive or irrational behavior.

THE DANGERS OF SPEEDBALLS

A speedball is a mixture of cocaine and heroin. Cocaine is a stimulant. Heroin is an opiate and a depressant. When taken at the same time, the drugs work together, which amplifies their effect. Users experience a more intense and rapid high than they would get from injecting either cocaine or heroin on its own, followed by a longer-lasting sense of happiness and euphoria. They feel less anxious and less tired, but more relaxed. The consequences, however, can be catastrophic. Taking stimulants with opiates can cause respiratory failure, stroke, or heart attack.

NEARLY DESTROYED BY CRACK

Thirty-one-year-old Araminta Jonsson of London, England, had firsthand experience with the devastating effects of crack. Her drug problems began in high school. She started drinking when she was just 13 years old. Soon, she moved on to illegal substances. By the time she was in college, she was doing cocaine on a regular basis to boost her confidence. "I'd get out of control, get into a relationship and feel good about myself for a little bit, then that would stop working and I'd pick up drugs or alcohol again. That would be the pattern," she told BBC News.[8]

Crack got its name because of the cracking sound the cocaine rocks make when they are heated.

After graduate school, Jonsson moved to Colombia, South America. She told herself it was because she wanted to write a book. But the real reason was to fuel her cocaine habit. Her dependency on coke got worse. She ended up in the hospital and had to be flown home, back to London, for treatment. When she found out she was pregnant, Jonsson stopped using briefly, only to start up again after the baby was born.

Eventually, Jonsson checked herself into a drug rehabilitation center. But instead of learning how to get clean, she started dating a man who was also in the program. Before long, the two were smoking crack together. The relationship quickly became physically and emotionally abusive. "I love my son, but the idea of my son or a crack pipe—I couldn't not choose the crack pipe," Jonsson said.[9]

COCAINE AND CRACK USE AMONG TEENS

According to the 2016 Monitoring the Future Study, a research initiative funded by the National Institute on Drug Abuse that analyzed drug use among American young adults, teen cocaine use has been on the decline since 2006.[11] The statistics reveal, however, that cocaine and crack use is still a real threat among middle and high school students.

- In 2016, an estimated 1.9 million people age 12 and older had used cocaine in the last month, and 432,000 people age 12 and older had used crack in the past month.
- About 0.8 percent of eighth graders said they had tried cocaine at least once in their lifetime, while 0.9 percent had tried crack.
- About 2.1 percent of high school sophomores said they had tried cocaine at least once in their lifetime, while 0.8 percent had tried crack.
- About 3.7 percent of high school seniors said they had tried cocaine at least once in their lifetime, while 1.4 percent had tried crack.

Eventually, Jonsson was able to extricate herself from that relationship. Today, she is finally living drug free. She runs *Pipe Down*, a magazine geared toward people with drug addictions, written by people with drug addictions. She says her work gives her a reason to get out of bed in the morning—a much-needed sense of purpose.

"People could say 'you've got your son, you've got your family' and yes, I have all that, but I needed something that filled my self-esteem, something that gave me self-worth," Jonsson told BBC News. "[Now] I'm being given that by regularly contributing to this magazine and, hopefully, doing something that's going to help other people."[10]

For many like Jonsson, crack and cocaine dependency is a seemingly unbeatable problem.

But the drug wasn't always viewed as unsafe. In fact, it has a fascinating history. From the rolling hills of South America to the laboratory, the therapist's couch, and supermarket shelves, cocaine in its different forms has captivated the people who encounter it for millennia.

Crack smoke loses its strength quickly, so the pipes are often short and may cause users to develop blisters and burns referred to as "crack lip."

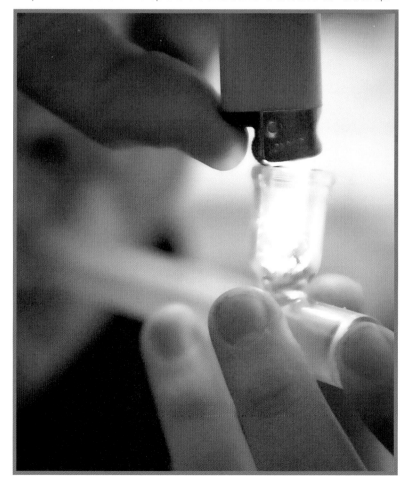

COCAINE'S ORIGINS

Cocaine use throughout the world has a complicated history. As far back as 1000 BCE in parts of Peru, Bolivia, and Colombia, people cultivated the coca plant, the source of cocaine. The bush grew on the lush eastern slopes of the Andes Mountains and in the dense woods of the Amazon Rainforest. In Peru, the indigenous people known as the Inca grew and harvested the plant to use in religious ceremonies. Members of the Inca nobility chewed coca leaves as a mild stimulant. Only a tiny amount of actual cocaine was in each leaf, so addiction wasn't really an issue.

In 1532, Spanish conquistador Francisco Pizarro led a campaign to topple the Incas, who ruled the largest empire in the Americas. He did so with the help of the coca bush. Knowing

Coca plants are native to South America and grow well on the slopes of the Andes Mountains.

how much the Incas valued coca leaves, he used the plant as a type of bribe to keep the Inca natives in line once they were conquered and under his control. Instead of paying them money for the grueling labor that he and the other conquistadors forced them to perform—building roads, mining, farming—Pizarro plied the Incas with coca leaves.

Soon, coca consumption wasn't just an Inca habit. Even the Spanish colonists in Peru chewed coca leaves. The Spanish took over the farming of coca bushes and planted them in mass quantities. They also brought the leaves back to Europe on ships. It was there, centuries later, that a German chemist heard about the plant and took its use to a whole new level.

In Inca religious ceremonies, the coca leaf was viewed as a symbol of life, fertility, strength, and power.

SCIENTIFIC BREAKTHROUGHS

Prior to the 1800s, the effects of cocaine could be accessed only by keeping the leaves intact and either chewing them directly or brewing coca tea. But in 1859, everything changed. That year, German chemist Albert Niemann made a groundbreaking discovery. He became the first person in the world to separate a stimulating powder from the coca plant. He called it *cocaina*. "Its solutions have an alkaline reaction, a bitter taste, promote the flow of saliva and leave a peculiar numbness, followed by a

THE BENEFITS OF COCA LEAVES

Cocaine makes up less than 1 percent of the coca bush.[2] When chewed or brewed as tea, the plant's leaves have noticeable positive effects. Coca leaves relieve nausea and dizziness. They can calm jittery nerves, settle an upset stomach, and keep hunger or thirst at bay. In addition to battling fatigue, chewed-up coca leaves can also cure altitude sickness.

sense of cold when applied to the tongue," Niemann wrote in his doctoral thesis, published in 1860.[1]

A year after his paper was published, Niemann died suddenly of unknown causes. Almost immediately, his former student, Wilhelm Lossen, continued Niemann's line of study. In 1865, Lossen figured out and published the chemical formula for cocaine—$C_{17}H_{21}NO_4$.

For nearly two decades afterward, scientists and doctors experimented with this newfound knowledge. They wanted to see what the newly discovered drug could do to advance the field of medicine.

Then, in the early 1880s, two more scientific breakthroughs occurred. Doctors discovered new uses for cocaine. One of these uses was as an anesthetic in eye surgeries. At the time, eye surgery was a brutal endeavor. Local anesthesia had not yet been invented, so patients would be forced to endure the pain of having cataracts removed without the benefit of a numbing agent. In 1884, Czechoslovakian ophthalmologist Carl Koller discovered that placing a couple drops of a cocaine-infused liquid in the eye could numb the eyeball so patients wouldn't feel the pain as intensely. Koller's discovery proved to be a gateway to the use of anesthetics in modern medicine.

Around the same time, 28-year-old Viennese neurologist Dr. Sigmund Freud became fascinated by cocaine's potential. He had read a paper written by Dr. Theodor Aschenbrandt, a German army physician who used cocaine to help soldiers stay strong during military drills. Freud was plagued by depression, neuroses, and chronic fatigue. He hoped using cocaine might alleviate not only his own ailments but also those of his patients.

"I have been reading about cocaine, the essential constituent of coca leaves, which some Indian tribes chew to enable them to resist privations and hardships," Freud wrote in a letter to his fiancée, Martha Bernays, on April 21, 1884. "I am procuring some myself and will try it with cases of heart disease and also of nervous exhaustion."[3]

WHO WAS FIRST?

German chemist Albert Niemann usually receives credit for isolating cocaine, but some historians insist Enrique Pizzi was truly responsible for the breakthrough. Pizzi was a professor of chemistry and pharmacology at the University of La Paz in Bolivia. In 1857, he conducted a series of experiments on coca leaves and was able to extract a fine white powder. Niemann tested Pizzi's sample and said it was gypsum, not cocaine. But 30 years later, a successor of Pizzi's tested the sample again to determine the truth. His findings showed that Niemann's assessment was incorrect. He concluded that Pizzi's sample was, indeed, cocaine. To this day, the issue of which chemist was first is still hotly debated.

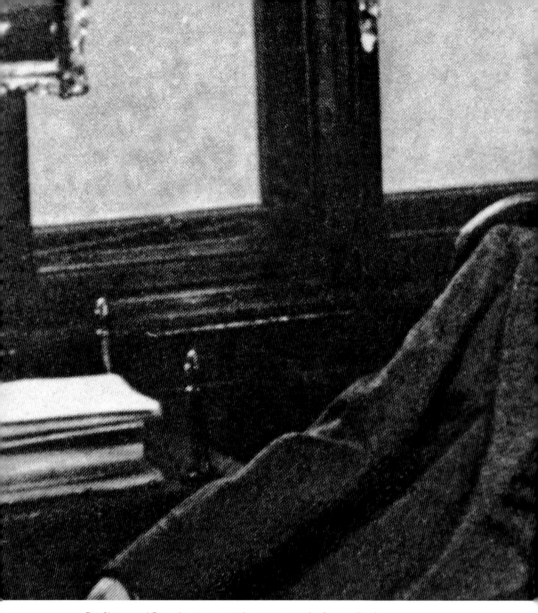

Dr. Sigmund Freud was an early proponent of cocaine's medical benefits.

As soon as Freud tried cocaine, he became convinced of cocaine's medical potential. That same year, he published a paper on the wonders of the miracle drug, titled *On Coca*. In it, he recommended the drug be taken orally. He used it to treat digestive disorders and asthma and also recommended

it as a mental stimulant and a possible treatment for morphine or alcohol addiction. Before long, Freud was taking cocaine regularly and prescribing it to his fiancée and many of his patients.

The medical community's response to Freud's paper—and some of the other cocaine-related scientific studies going on at the time—was overwhelmingly positive. Pharmaceutical companies started manufacturing the drug in large quantities. It was the new hot drug, and everyone wanted a piece of the profits.

HOW IS COCAINE MADE?

In the 1880s, the methods used to produce cocaine were arduous and took a long time. The process has changed little since. First, workers plucked the coca leaves and separated the leaves into piles. Next, they chopped up the leaves and dried them, which was an important step. If the leaves were moist at this point in the manufacturing process, they would rot and contaminate the batch.

Workers then coated the dried leaves with cement powder, which was used as a

It takes approximately one metric ton of coca leaves—approximately 2,200 pounds—to make a kilogram of paste, which can be turned around and sold for about $900.[4]

A worker sprinkles cement over mulched coca leaves at a makeshift lab in Antioquia, Colombia.

thickening agent. The leaves were placed in large barrels and mixed with other additives such as gasoline, ammonia, sulfuric acid, and sodium permanganate until a thick paste formed. At this stage, workers often wore masks because the stench was overwhelming.

THE TRUTH ABOUT COCA COLA

America's favorite soda is named *Coca Cola* for a reason. One of the main ingredients of early versions of the drink was, in fact, cocaine. In the early 1880s, American pharmacist John Stith Pemberton set about making his own version of Vin Mariani by mixing cocaine and wine. He called it Pemberton's French Wine Cola. But when his home county in Georgia passed a law outlawing alcohol, Pemberton changed the recipe. He replaced the wine with sugar syrup. He called it Coca-Cola: The Temperance Drink.

At first, the drink was sold in whites-only segregated soda fountains. But in 1899, Pemberton's company started selling the beverage in bottles. Everyone could buy it, including African Americans. White people—especially wealthy whites—were not pleased. Newspapers in the South reported that "negro cocaine fiends" were causing trouble in communities. Because of this racist sentiment, as well as the passage of anti-narcotics laws at the turn of the 1900s, all traces of cocaine were removed from the soft drink.

Finally, when the paste was ready, it was cooked under a medium heat until most of the water and chemicals evaporated. The paste was then crushed, packed into a mold, and cut into pieces small enough to be packaged and sold. Later, this same paste would be combined with diluted sulfuric acid and potassium permanganate and filtered. The paste was then mixed with ammonia, filtered again, and dried to produce cocaine hydrochloride—the powdery white substance that gets distributed on the street.

Despite the laborious manufacturing process, by the early 1900s, cocaine use had skyrocketed. In a period of less than two decades, five times as many people were doing the drug. By that time, over-the-counter medicines with

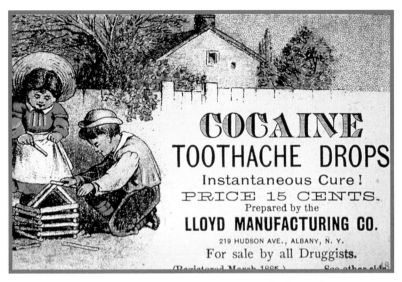

Some early over-the-counter medications promoted cocaine as an effective ingredient. At the time, few people realized how dangerous and addictive cocaine could be.

cocaine in them, such as toothache drops, had been approved by medical boards. What followed next was inevitable. Many people, including Freud, reported cocaine addictions.

Governments worldwide needed to do something about the spreading epidemic. In 1914, Congress passed a bill targeting the cocaine problem in the United States. The Harrison Narcotics Tax Act taxed all people who "produce, import, manufacture, compound, deal in, dispense, sell, distribute, or give away" coca leaves or cocaine in any form.[5] The law affected not only everyday users but also pharmaceutical companies and doctors. It was the first bill of its kind to be passed in the United States. But it would not be the last.

CHAPTER FOUR

COCAINE AND THE LAW

On April 12, 2017, Cassandra Sainsbury planned to fly from Bogotá, Colombia, to Hong Kong, China. But she never got on the plane. The 22-year-old Australian was stopped at an immigration checkpoint at Bogotá's El Dorado International Airport. When police searched Sainsbury's luggage, they uncovered nearly 13 pounds (6 kg) of cocaine hidden in 18 headphone cases.[1] She was immediately arrested and put in one of Colombia's most notorious, overcrowded prisons: El Buen Pastor.

"I found myself in a bad situation and I suppose I couldn't find a way out," Sainsbury told the television news show *60 Minutes* in an interview five months after her arrest. "I was in a

An X-ray machine at the airport in Bogotá, Colombia, detected the cocaine stashed in Cassandra Sainsbury's luggage.

place where I didn't know who I could trust, who I could talk to, and so I sort of just went with what I was told to do."[2]

Sainsbury insists she didn't originally know she would be transporting drugs. Instead, she claims that when she was in Australia and looking for jobs, she had responded to a classified ad posted on the internet. She was hired as a courier to shuttle secret documents from Colombia to Hong Kong. In return, she was supposed to receive $10,000 in cash. "I was at the point where I needed money. So, I thought 'OK. I'll do it,'" Sainsbury said.[3]

The 5.8 kilos confiscated from Cassie Sainsbury's luggage had a street value of nearly $2 million.[5]

What followed after Sainsbury accepted the assignment was typical to many drug smuggling cases: nothing was as it had originally seemed. Sainsbury was flown from her home in Australia to China, then to the United States, and finally to Colombia. She was told to stay at a specific hotel, where she met a man named Angelo, who set the trafficking plan in motion. When Sainsbury realized she would be carrying cocaine, not documents, she reportedly told Angelo she wanted out. Unfortunately, extricating herself from the situation wasn't an option. "Basically, [Angelo] told me that if I didn't go through and do the job and take the package, that my mum, my sister, and my partner—they would be killed," Sainsbury said.[4]

"COCAINE CASSIE"

By the time Sainsbury ended up at the Colombia airport, the US Drug Enforcement Administration (DEA) had already gotten involved. Her complicated flight route had raised red flags with the US Transportation Security Administration (TSA). The TSA informed the DEA, which warned Colombian authorities of Sainsbury's departure. The airport police promptly intercepted her.

In the months after her arrest, as she awaited her trial, Sainsbury was bullied at El Buen Pastor. Though she originally faced a minimum of 21 years in prison, her lawyer offered her a plea deal. In exchange for admitting she was solely responsible for the crime, her sentence would be reduced to six years.

A police officer escorts Sainsbury to a court hearing in Bogotá, Colombia.

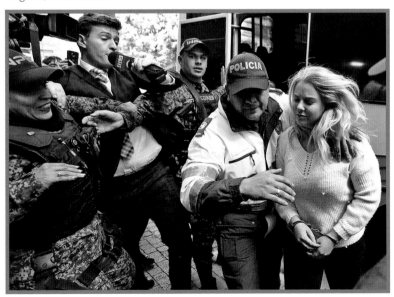

COCAINE TRAFFICKING

UNITED STATES

UNITED STATES

NORTH ATLANTIC OCEAN

MEXICO

CARIBBEAN

CENTRAL AMERICA

NORTH PACIFIC OCEAN

VENEZUELA

GUYANA

SURINAME

FRENCH GUIANA

COLOMBIA

ECUADOR

N
W E
S

PERU

BRAZIL

SOUTH PACIFIC OCEAN

BOLIVIA

PARAGUAY

URUGUAY

CHILE

ARGENTINA

Cocaine is trafficked from South America to countries all over the world.

WESTERN AND CENTRAL EUROPE

SPAIN

WEST AFRICA

INDIAN OCEAN

SOUTH ATLANTIC OCEAN

In late October, Sainsbury accepted the deal in court. She agreed to a six-year prison term and a fine of $90,000. News reports stated "Cocaine Cassie" could be released in as little as three years with good behavior. "I suppose I took the risk. Now I'm [in prison]," Sainsbury told *60 Minutes*. "It's a lesson learned. Definitely."[6]

COCAINE IN AMERICA

Sainsbury's experience trafficking drugs out of Colombia is a sobering reminder of the types of serious problems the country faces. In recent years, Colombia's cocaine output has ballooned to record-setting highs. In 2015, farmers cultivated and harvested nearly 400,000 acres (162,000 ha) of coca plants, doubling production since 2013.[7] That's twice as much as Peru and Bolivia's outputs combined.

After the coca crop is harvested, much of it is trafficked or smuggled to other countries. A large portion of Colombia's massive cocaine output is headed for the United States. The United States is the third-highest cocaine-consuming country per person in the world, after Albania and Scotland. A

DRUG SMUGGLING

Drug traffickers smuggle illegal drugs in and out of a country in exchange for large sums of money. According to the US Sentencing Commission, in 2016 authorities recorded 19,222 drug trafficking cases in the United States. Nearly 20 percent of those were related to cocaine seizures, and about 8 percent were crack related.[8]

2017 annual report on the global narcotics trade released by the US State Department states that 90 percent of the cocaine for sale in the United States comes from Colombia.[9] A bumper crop in Colombia means even more cocaine on the streets in the United States. "There are troubling early signs that cocaine use and availability is on the rise in the United States for the first time in nearly a decade," the State Department noted in its 2017 report.[10]

According to the US Substance Abuse and Mental Health Services Administration (SAMHSA), more young adults and college-age students are using cocaine too. Between 2013 and 2015, the number of young people who had tried cocaine for the first time increased 61 percent, from 601,000 to 968,000.[11] About 1 in 20 adults between the ages of 18 and 25 used the drug in 2015, with the highest percentage living in the northeastern part of

COCAINE ERADICATION

For Colombians, the production of coca plants is complicated. Many farmers rely on profits from the harvested crop to survive. But Colombia's government had to take action to stop the massive flow of cocaine out of the country. Its leaders initiated a full-scale eradication program. At first, pilots flew over fields and sprayed the coca plants with herbicides. Later, the government took a more aggressive approach. They sent teams of workers into the fields to rip up the coca plants by hand. The tactics haven't been totally successful. Farmers block roads leading to the plants to stop their crops from being ruined. Some farm owners have even planted bombs among the coca bushes to prevent government workers from doing more damage.

the United States.[12] With the increase in coca crop production, these numbers may go up. The result could mean more cocaine addicts, more narcotic cops on the street, more arrests, and more people in jail for drug-related crimes.

"We are working the problem. It is a serious problem. Both governments recognize this fact," said William Brownfield, the assistant secretary of the State Department's Bureau of International Narcotics and Law Enforcement Affairs. "Both governments realize that it is neither in the interest of Colombia, nor in the United States of America, nor, frankly, any country in the Western Hemisphere or the world, that there be more than a doubling of cocaine production."[13]

SERIOUS PUNISHMENT

With the rise of cocaine use in the United States, it is imperative that mental health workers and police forces are even more vigilant about confronting people with drug addictions. Many certified drug counselors emphasize the need for adequate inpatient and outpatient treatment programs for addicts. Lawmakers are working with police officers to apprehend and prosecute addicts for drug-related crimes. The federal government is also cracking down on drug use in the United States. Since Congress passed the Harrison Narcotics Tax Act in 1914, a number of laws have shaped US drug policy—some with unintended consequences.

On October 27, 1970, President Richard Nixon signed the Controlled Substances Act.

The most influential law was the Controlled Substances Act of 1970, signed into law by President Richard Nixon. The law regulated the manufacturing, trafficking, possession, sale, and use of controlled substances. The act covered a variety of substances, from over-the-counter medications to stronger drugs such as hallucinogens, narcotics, depressants, and stimulants. It also divided these drugs into separate categories called schedules. A drug's level of potential addictiveness, its medical benefits, and its safety in use determined which schedule the drug was classified under, with Schedule I being the most controlled and Schedule V being the least strictly regulated.

In 1973, President Nixon created the DEA. Its task is to enforce the Controlled Substances Act by investigating and prosecuting cases that violate the act's rules. The DEA also seizes any illegal drugs that come into the country via smugglers

DRUG SCHEDULES

Under the Controlled Substances Act of 1970, there are five categories, or schedules, of drugs. Schedule I drugs are the most harmful and were determined to not have any medical benefits. The categories, and examples of the drugs in each category, are as follows:

- Schedule I: Heroin, LSD, Ecstasy, Marijuana, Peyote
- Schedule II: Cocaine, Morphine, Methamphetamine, Ritalin, OxyContin
- Schedule III: Anabolic Steroids, Ketamine, Vicodin, Marinol
- Schedule IV: Ambien, Xanax, Valium, Ativan
- Schedule V: Lyrica, Cough Suppressants, Antidiarrheal Drugs

and works with the United Nations and other groups on matters relating to international drug-control programs.

Under the Controlled Substances Act, cocaine is categorized as a Schedule II drug. According to the DEA, Schedule II drugs are defined as "drugs with a high potential for abuse, with use potentially leading to severe psychological or physical dependence."[14] Because of the Schedule II classification, cocaine users receive a significant punishment if they are caught doing or selling any quantity of the drug. For example, a first-time offender caught with anywhere from 500 to 4,999 grams of cocaine, which is approximately 1 to 11 pounds, can be punished with at least 5 years in prison and a fine of up to $5 million, according to the DEA's rules.[15]

While every US state prohibits the trafficking, sale, and possession of cocaine, Schedule II–related charges vary state by state. For example, if a repeat offender is arrested for having cocaine in Oregon, it is considered a Class C felony. This type of felony has a maximum prison sentence of 5 years and a maximum fine of $125,000.[16] If someone is caught manufacturing or selling cocaine, it is a Class B felony. These felonies have a maximum prison sentence of 10 years and a fine of up to $250,000.[17]

Whatever the situation, buying or selling cocaine is considered a serious offense in the United States. Aside from causing legal problems, cocaine is also extraordinarily detrimental to a user's health. It is one of the most dangerous drugs on the market, with devastating effects on the brain and body.

CRACK AND RACE

In 1986, Congress passed the Anti-Drug Abuse Act. It established mandatory prison sentences for drug offenses. Some people complained about the law's 100:1 ratio in the sentencing guidelines for crack and cocaine offenses. For example, a person caught with 5 grams of crack faces a minimum sentence of 5 years in prison. To receive the exact same sentence, a person would need to possess 500 grams of powdered cocaine.

Crack was cheaper and used more often by African Americans in lower-income neighborhoods. Powdered cocaine was expensive and used more often by wealthy white Americans in affluent neighborhoods. Consequently, more African Americans were thrown in jail for first-time drug offenses than whites.

According to the US Sentencing Commission, in 2009, 79 percent of 5,669 sentenced crack offenders were black. About 10 percent were white and 10 percent were Hispanic. In contrast, there were 6,020 powdered cocaine cases. Of those, 17 percent of offenders were white, 28 percent were black, and 53 percent were Hispanic.[18]

COCAINE AND THE BRAIN

Cocaine is one of the most popular party drugs in the United States. Users report feeling upbeat, confident, and more alert even after the first bump. But those positive feelings come at a cost. Cocaine impacts the way the brain normally functions, resulting in serious and permanent damage.

The brain is a complex network that enables the body to move and feel sensations. The brain contains billions of nerve cells, called neurons. Each neuron has two branches that extend outward from the cell body. One branch is called an axon. It sends messages from the nerve cell body to neurons or muscle cells nearby. The other branch is called a dendrite. Dendrites

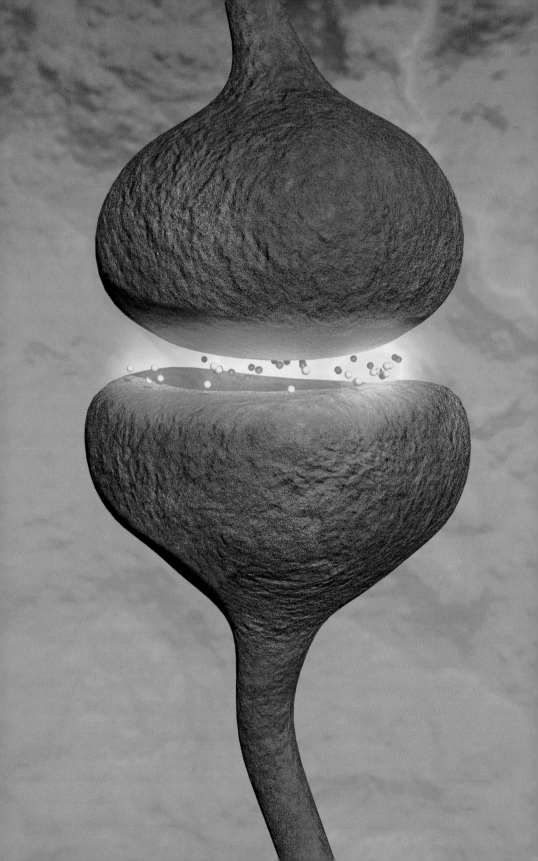

receive messages from other nerve cells. Axons and dendrites allow neurons to communicate with each other and with other cells in the body.

The process begins when neurons are stimulated. They send an electrical signal to other cells in the area. When an activated neuron sends an electrical signal from its cell body to the end of its axon, the signal reaches a synapse. At the synapse, the incoming electrical impulse triggers the release of chemicals called neurotransmitters. These neurotransmitters travel across the synapse from the first nerve cell and attach to receptors on the other half of the synapse located on a dendrite of a neighboring nerve cell. This process repeats itself, from neuron to neuron, until the message is received at its destination. When this system is working properly, the brain can coordinate behavior, emotion, sensation, thought, and movement.

Neurotransmitters are an essential part of the brain's limbic system. The limbic system controls and regulates the body's ability to experience emotions and feel pleasure. It does this by using a neurotransmitter called dopamine. The brain releases dopamine when a person has pleasurable experiences. Running, doing yoga, spending time with friends, and even eating a delicious slice of cherry pie are all examples of activities that might release dopamine.

Under normal circumstances, the release of dopamine encourages the body to repeat behaviors that keep it feeling great and strong. The more pleasure a person feels, the more likely he or she is to repeat the behavior. This is sometimes called the brain's reward circuit. In a cocaine user's brain, the reward circuit operates in an entirely different fashion. It doesn't function like it is supposed to.

SHORT-TERM EFFECTS

In a sober person's brain, dopamine travels from one neuron to another, then back to the original nerve cell to be recycled and used again. But in a cocaine user's brain, this doesn't happen. When cocaine is snorted or crack is inhaled through a pipe, the drug makes its way from the nose, throat, or lungs to the brain. There, it blocks the dopamine transporters. This prevents dopamine from being picked up and recycled. Consequently, dopamine accumulates in the synapses of nerve cells, which triggers what users experience as a high.

"The transporter is like a pump in a swimming pool that recycles water to keep the water at a certain level," explains Dr. Steve Grant, a scientist who works for the National Institute on Drug Abuse. "Cocaine clogs the pump, allowing dopamine levels to rise to abnormally high levels, just like a clogged water pump will make a swimming pool overflow and produce a flood."[1]

In the short term, a dopamine buildup between nerve cells in the reward system has all sorts of effects on the brain, many of which might appear positive. Some people like using cocaine because it helps them feel more outgoing and boosts their self-confidence. Other people—especially college students—report the drug helps them feel awake and alert. Thanks to cocaine, they are able stay up all night studying for an exam or chatting with friends. The excess dopamine in the brain is responsible for a sense of bliss and euphoria.

Unfortunately, there are immediate downsides to using cocaine, mostly because the brain is on overdrive. Even someone who tries cocaine for the first time can become hypersensitive to light, sound, and touch. Normal noises like crickets chirping or a finger tapping on a desk might seem overwhelming and too loud to handle. Frequent cocaine users can also become paranoid.

DOPAMINE AND TOLERANCE

When the brain experiences excess dopamine for long periods, it becomes tolerant of the elevated levels and lowers the amount of dopamine it produces. People with a cocaine tolerance no longer feel the pleasurable effects of increased dopamine. To bring dopamine levels back up to normal—and feel even a small amount of happiness—they need do a larger amount of cocaine to override their tolerance. Incapacitating crashes can occur when people with a cocaine tolerance stop taking the drug. They feel depressed or even numb. To counteract the crash, they take even larger amounts of cocaine. This cycle is called addiction, and it is very difficult to break.

THE BRAIN'S REWARD CIRCUIT

In a healthy person's brain, dopamine is released whenever pleasure is experienced by the body. It sends the brain reward signals and prompts the body to repeat the activity in order to get another pleasurable response. Dopamine is produced in an area of the midbrain called the ventral tegmental area (VTA) and sent to other parts of the brain. Each part is controlled by dopamine levels, and each has a specific function that using cocaine alters or hinders.

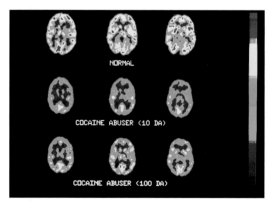

A PET scan shows the effects of cocaine on the brain. The sober brain (top) has patches of red and yellow, which are signs of healthy activity. Cocaine reduces this activity at the time of use, ten days after use (center), and even 100 days after use (bottom).

The brain's reward circuit powerfully motivates behaviors, and it plays a vital role in understanding why people become addicted to drugs.

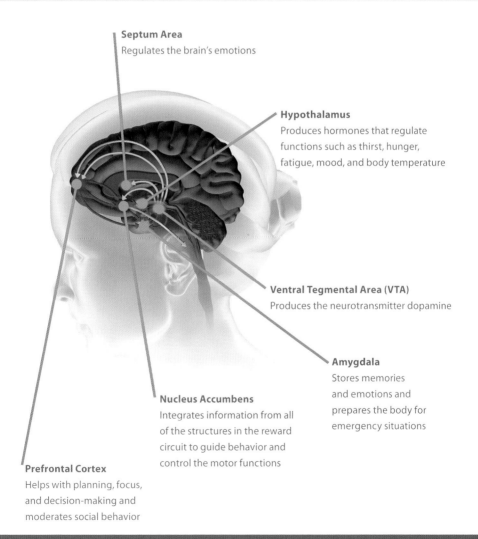

Septum Area
Regulates the brain's emotions

Hypothalamus
Produces hormones that regulate functions such as thirst, hunger, fatigue, mood, and body temperature

Ventral Tegmental Area (VTA)
Produces the neurotransmitter dopamine

Amygdala
Stores memories and emotions and prepares the body for emergency situations

Nucleus Accumbens
Integrates information from all of the structures in the reward circuit to guide behavior and control the motor functions

Prefrontal Cortex
Helps with planning, focus, and decision-making and moderates social behavior

A condition known as anhedonia happens when a person is no longer motivated to take part in activities he or she used to enjoy. This joyless state is caused by a decrease in dopamine.

"WHAT DO YOU MEAN I'M PARANOID?"

Between 68 and 84 percent of cocaine users experience paranoia.[3] It is a mental disorder with symptoms that include anxiety, feelings of confusion or distrust, and cognitive impairment. In mild cases, paranoia can spark irrational thoughts or beliefs. For example, a man might become convinced that the cops are waiting outside his house, even though all evidence points to that not being true. In more extreme cases, cocaine can cause mental or visual delusions. For example, a woman might think aliens have orchestrated a nationwide plot against her, or she might believe elephants are climbing up her bedroom wall.

They might experience a range of emotions, including irritability, anxiety, or defensiveness.

LONG-TERM EFFECTS

Cocaine's short-term effects on the brain are troublesome. But the drug's long-term effects can be devastating. The most obvious consequence to using cocaine repeatedly over a long period of time is the high probability of addiction, a brain disease that occurs when a person uses a drug compulsively, despite negative consequences, and becomes dependent on a drug in order to function normally.

"Many cocaine users report that they have less ability to experience pleasure in life," explains Dr. David Gorelick of the National Institute on Drug Abuse.[2] In other words,

People who are addicted to cocaine have trouble with everyday tasks such as concentrating at school or controlling impulses.

they become tolerant of the drug and must go back for more again and again in order to feel the same euphoric high they experienced the first time around.

Prolonged cocaine use has a number of other side effects, most of which affect a person's personality and are nearly impossible to reverse. Though many people start taking cocaine to improve their concentration, chronic cocaine users often suffer from a lack of focus. They have a difficult time making decisions and keeping impulses in check. Some experience foul moods and complain of an inability to prevent harmful thoughts from

The side effects of cocaine usage can be so disagreeable that users may take cocaine again to ease the symptoms, creating a destructive pattern.

flooding their brain at random or unexpected moments. Other long-lasting side effects include insomnia, panic attacks, and psychosis. Cocaine addiction can also spark extremely violent behavior. Many addicts will then take more cocaine to relieve these negative side effects, fueling a dangerous negative spiral that can seem nearly impossible to climb out of.

No matter if it's the first time or the fifty-first, coming into contact with any form of cocaine—whether it's powder, freebase cocaine, or crack—leaves the brain permanently altered. It also affects the body. Snorting, inhaling, or injecting the drug not only impairs the body's organs but also can cause them to fail altogether.

A COMEBACK FROM ADDICTION

Robert Downey Jr. is one of the most sought-after actors in the movie business. After starring in Marvel's mega-popular Iron Man franchise, he became one of the top-earning actors in Hollywood. But Downey wasn't always on top of his game. At one point in his career, he bottomed out, mostly because of drugs.

In 1996, Downey was arrested for speeding. The cops searched the car and found cocaine, crack, and heroin. From there, he cycled in and out of rehab for years, but nothing stuck. In 1999, he was sent to prison for cocaine possession and served just under a year. His friends staged interventions, but Downey refused to give up his habit. Finally, in 2003, Downey met producer Susan Levin on the set of Gothika. Soon after the two began a romantic relationship, Levin gave Downey an ultimatum: me or drugs. The tactic worked. On July 4, 2003, Downey threw his drugs in the Pacific Ocean and decided he was done for good. He has been successful ever since.

CHAPTER SIX

COCAINE AND THE BODY

Malcolm Thaler is a physician with One Medical Group in New York City. He treats a lot of people with a variety of health concerns, including the common cold, back pain, and the flu. He also sees patients with persistent drug habits. Out of all the recreational drugs on the market, the one he cautions his patients against the most is cocaine.

"I think this is one drug where I can safely say there's no guarantee," Thaler explains. "It only takes one time to get a lethal heart arrhythmia or seizure. It doesn't matter whether it's your hundredth time [doing it] or your first time, it's just not safe."[1]

In 2011, emergency departments saw 1.2 million visits related to illegal drug use. Nearly one-half of those visits were to treat people who had used cocaine.

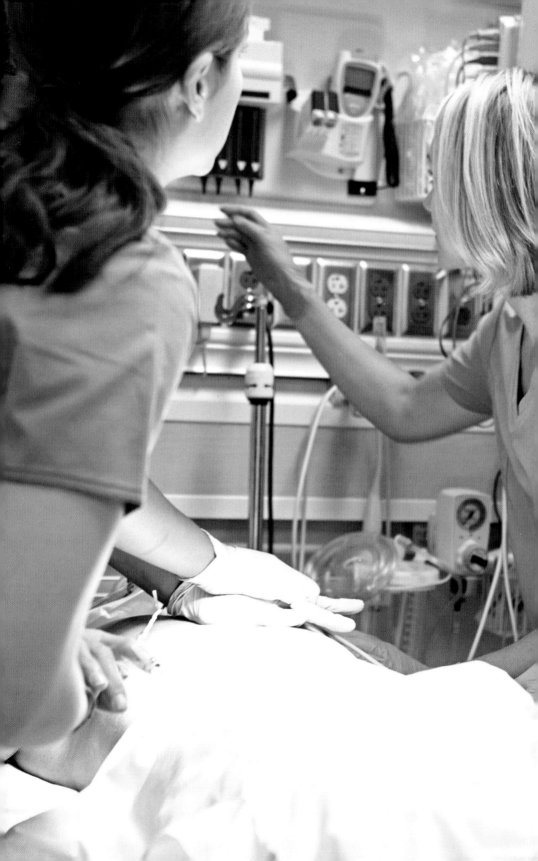

LEVAMISOLE'S FLESH-EATING PROPERTIES

Levamisole, a drug used to deworm cattle, is found in approximately 65 percent of cocaine sold on the street.[3] Though the amount of levamisole in most stashes is too low to do any long-term harm to users, there are a few exceptions. If ingested in large quantities, levamisole can rot the skin and cause oozing sores on the legs, arms, and face. "(Some users) may be walking around like a time bomb," says Dr. Noah Craft of the Los Angeles Biomedical Research Institute. "About 10 percent of these patients will die from severe infections."[4]

Thaler isn't alone in his opinion. Dr. Ann Bolger, spokesperson for the American Heart Association, agrees with Thaler's assessment. In the many patients she sees with cocaine addictions, the main point she tries to drive home is just how lethal the drug can be, even for novice users.

"What I often try to explain to my patients who are stuck in this terrible situation where they become habituated to the use of cocaine . . . is that this is going to harm in a permanent way the biggest blood vessels in [their] body down to the smallest," Bolger says. "Every time [they are] exposed to cocaine, their heart is losing a little bit of muscle, and when that muscle dies, that little bit will never come back."[2]

Just as it impacts the brain, cocaine affects the body in a variety of ways. Some physical effects are short term. Others, like Dr. Bolger suggests, are irreversible.

SHORT-TERM EFFECTS

There are many physical signs of cocaine use. Some are instantly recognizable. The most obvious symptom is dilated, or widened, pupils. "Cocaine [use leads] to the pupils' delayed or lack of reaction to light," says toxicologist Thorsten Binschenck-Domass. "These symptoms can outlast the subjective effect of the substance for many hours and up to two days. They may also lead to an enhanced sensitivity to glare."[5]

Bruxism—excessive teeth grinding or jaw clenching—is also common, causing damage to the jawbone. When cocaine is inhaled through the nose, some of it slips down the back of the throat and mixes with saliva. This forms an acidic substance that dissolves teeth enamel and eventually creates cavities. Mouth ulcers can also take root in the gums. A person high on cocaine may also act jittery, become anxious, or talk a lot. Other physical signs of cocaine use include increased body temperature, heart rate, and blood pressure. Some cocaine users also report nausea, dizziness, and tremors.

For people who snort cocaine, the body part that receives the most damage—at least on the surface—is the nose. Coke addicts often have a chronically inflamed, runny nose. Frequent cocaine use can lead to nosebleeds and an inability to smell. It can also irritate the nasal septum, which is the bridge between the nostrils. In the most serious cases, harsh chemicals

When a person snorts cocaine, the mucous membranes in the nose absorb the drug. This can cause sneezing, nasal congestion, a runny nose, and nosebleeds.

in the cocaine eat away at the septum until it collapses or disintegrates altogether.

Because the nasal cavity is connected to the throat, many users, especially those who smoke and inhale crack, complain of a sore throat. They may have problems swallowing. Some develop hoarseness or a hacking cough. In more serious cases, adult-onset asthma is possible.

Just as heroin users do, people who inject cocaine into their veins get unattractive marks called tracks on their arms, between their toes, or wherever they inject the drug. If not cared for properly, these wounds can become sore, get infected, and fester. Like any drug user who uses needles, cocaine injectors are also at greater risk for blood-borne diseases such as HIV/AIDS or Hepatitis C.

LONG-TERM EFFECTS

While the short-term physical effects of cocaine abuse are debilitating, the long-term effects of cocaine can be lethal. Cocaine damages most of the organs in the body. First and foremost, it attacks the heart. Whether snorted, smoked, or injected, cocaine narrows the blood vessels, so the heart has to work much harder to push blood to the rest of the body. This increases the risk of stroke, inflammation of the heart muscle, and aortic ruptures. Any of these conditions can be fatal.

COCAINE AND PREGNANCY RISKS

According to most doctors, pregnant women should never do recreational drugs, even alcohol. This is because the drugs they consume pass directly to the baby inside the womb. Yet the National Institute on Drug Abuse reports that more than 750,000 pregnancies are exposed to cocaine every year.[7] Taking any amount of cocaine poses significant risks to the mother. Among other consequences, pregnant users can experience problems such as migraines or the separation of the placental lining from the uterus. They also have a higher risk of premature delivery or even miscarriage.

Babies born to mothers who use cocaine are rarely healthy because their liver and other organs are not developed enough to detoxify the drug. Many have respiratory ailments, low birth weight, and, in some cases, smaller heads. Some suffer from behavioral problems and learning disabilities later in life. In extreme cases, babies inherit a cocaine addiction from their mothers and have to go through treatment to be weaned off the drug's effects.

"Cocaine increases the amount of oxygen needed by the heart because it stimulates the heart to beat faster and stronger," explains National Institute on Drug Abuse's Dr. Gorelick. "At the same time, [it decreases] the amount of blood flowing to the heart muscle, or [blocks] blood flow completely."[6]

In addition to the cardiovascular system, cocaine reduces the flow of blood in the gastrointestinal tract. This can cause ulcers in the stomach and liver. Chronic users often report a lack of appetite, which can lead to undesired weight loss. Malnutrition is common, as is a lowering of the body's metabolism, a collection of chemical reactions that occurs in the body to convert the fuel in food into energy the body needs to move and grow.

Other organs also suffer. Long-term cocaine use can cause bleeding in the brain, which increases the probability of stroke. Cocaine users are at a higher risk for disorders that affect the body's ability to move and function properly, such as Parkinson's disease. Inhaling crack also irritates the lining of the lungs. This causes painful swelling of the lung tissue and can lead to tumor growth and even cancer. But the worst side effect is death, which often happens because of an overdose.

OVERDOSING ON COCAINE

Most cocaine users want enough of the drug to get high without overdosing, and crossing that line is often unintentional. An overdose occurs when a person snorts, injects, or inhales too much of a drug and has a toxic reaction. Overdosing can cause heart attack, stroke, seizures, kidney failure, and bleeding in the brain. According to the

COCAINE, HIV/AIDS, AND HEPATITIS C

Some people who inject cocaine share needles to cut down on cost. The habit is extraordinarily dangerous. Infected intravenous drug users can spread deadly illnesses to uninfected users by sharing needles. Two of the most deadly diseases that are contracted directly through blood are HIV/AIDS and Hepatitis C.

The virus commonly known as HIV causes AIDS, a disease that slowly destroys the body's immune system. Hepatitis C is an infection that eats away at liver cells. According to the National Institute on Drug Abuse, cocaine use accelerates HIV infection by impairing immune cell function. If left untreated, Hepatitis C can cause cancer and multiple organ failure. Both AIDS and Hepatitis C can be fatal.

Centers for Disease Control and Prevention, of the estimated 64,000 US drug overdose deaths in 2016, more than 10,600 were cocaine related.[8]

A number of warning signs can help diagnose a potential drug overdose. Symptoms include elevated heart rate, irregular heartbeat, excessively high body temperature, and profuse sweating. People who mix cocaine with other dangerous drugs, such as heroin, methamphetamines, prescription drugs, or even alcohol, increase their risk of an overdose.

It is possible to fatally overdose the first time you try cocaine.

A cocaine overdose can happen to a person of any age, race, gender, economic status, state of physical fitness, or race or ethnicity. Retired Los Angeles Lakers basketball player Lamar Odom was one of those people. At the height of his career, he was using cocaine nearly every day. But one dark night in 2015, after doing copious amounts of cocaine, he was found unconscious at a nightclub. He had endured several strokes, and his kidneys had failed. He was in a coma and nearly died. After four days, he woke up in the hospital with tubes in his mouth and nose.

"When I woke up in the hospital room in Nevada, I couldn't move. I couldn't talk. I was trapped inside my own body," he later wrote in a piece for the *Players' Tribune*. "When you're an addict, nothing can get through to you. I never thought I was

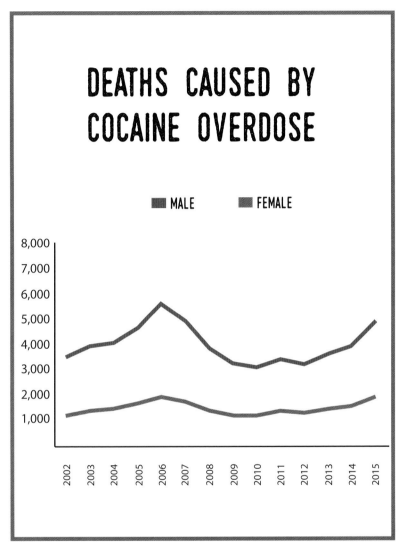

DEATHS CAUSED BY COCAINE OVERDOSE

■ MALE   ■ FEMALE

Between 2002 and 2015, men were more likely than women to die from a cocaine overdose.

going to die. I never thought I'd be in a coma. I didn't think I had

a problem. But then I woke up in a bed with tubes coming out of

my mouth—and it was real."[9]

Odom's 18-year-old daughter Destiny and 14-year-old son Lamar Jr. were fed up with their father's antics. They had tried to talk sense into him, but to no avail. After the overdose, they staged an intervention to make sure he got help. "I basically gave him the ultimatum that it was rehab or me not speaking to him anymore. I think it hit him really hard," Destiny told *People*. "When your parent is an addict and they get clean, it's like a whole new world—a whole new person, really. It's crazy what therapy and rehab can do to a person."[10]

OVERDOSE REVERSAL

The only way to prevent a cocaine overdose is to stop using the drug. But some scientists are working with doctors and mental health specialists to come up with ways to treat an overdose when it occurs. In 2012, a study published in the scientific journal *Molecular Pharmaceutics* described an injectable solution that could possibly reverse the effects of a cocaine overdose. The solution was made from artificially produced human antibodies. The antibodies isolate the cocaine and remove it from the body. So far, the experiment has only worked on mice. As of 2017, research is still ongoing.

CONSEQUENCES OF ADDICTION

In June 2017, *CBC News* published a harrowing article about a 58-year-old mother in Manitoba, Canada, who lost two children to drug addiction. Lois Fridfinnson had contacted the Canadian news outlet because she wanted to speak out about the trauma she endured. She hoped that by sharing her experiences, she might help other parents facing similar circumstances.

Fridfinnson's trouble started nearly two decades earlier. At the time, her youngest son, Michael, was just beginning to blossom socially and had lots of friends. He was acting and singing in local theater performances, and he was playing in rock bands around town. But when her son was

A loved one who is addicted to cocaine can affect the entire family deeply, bringing on high levels of stress, sadness, anger, and fear.

14, Fridfinnson found a lighter in Michael's pocket. She initially thought Michael was smoking cigarettes, but she later found out he was using marijuana. "It started changing his personality, and school started to be affected, friends started to change. You know, the signs were all there," she said.[1]

Fridfinnson approached a local addiction treatment center for help and was advised to use "tough love." A parents' group suggested she "let him hit rock-bottom."[2] The tactics backfired. Michael started sneaking around and lying about his whereabouts. By the time he turned 18, he had moved out of the house and was sleeping on friends' couches. He had also graduated to using more serious drugs, such as cocaine and crack.

According to the National Institute on Drug Abuse, alcohol and nicotine prime the brain for a heightened response to other drugs including cocaine and crack.

"I would say by 15 or 16, he was well into other drugs. You know, many say that marijuana is not the gateway for other drugs, and for some that may be true, but for Michael it was definitely a gateway into other drugs," Fridfinnson said.[3]

The uptick in cocaine and other drug use wrecked Michael's appearance and his social life. He lost a lot of weight and couldn't hold down a job. He started selling drugs and stealing in order to pay for his habit. For short periods of time, he even became homeless and lived on the street.

Despite a few short bouts in and out of rehab, nothing seemed to stick. Michael eventually ended up with a two-year jail term after robbing a gas station with some friends. Not long after his sentence ended, he met up with a friend from prison who was willing to share his methadone, an opioid medication used to treat serious drug addictions. Michael drank so much of it that his heart stopped.

Michael died on May 1, 2010, at the age of 23, just two days before he was scheduled to check himself in to a drug rehabilitation facility. Bricey, Michael's younger sister, died seven years later in March 2017, when she was 26. She lost a long battle with heart disease contracted after injecting herself

WHAT IS TOUGH LOVE?

"Tough love" means treating another person harshly—not to be mean, but to help them heal or inspire them to seek treatment. Many doctors, mental health advocates, and drug rehab staff members advocate using this approach to wean a loved one off a drug addiction, especially if other methods have not worked. Examples of tough love include:

- Stopping financial support, including providing an allowance, paying for bills, or lending money

- Taking away a phone or car that can be used to buy or sell drugs

- Breaking up a romantic relationship or friendship

- Not allowing the person with the drug problem in the home

- Calling the police or Child Protective Services

Teens experiment with cocaine for many reasons, including to appear popular, to ease loneliness, to fit in with friends, to erase boredom, or to get back at parents or guardians.

Cocaine addiction and the behaviors associated with it can lead to prison time.

with illegal drugs using dirty needles. The siblings' mother is still

mourning the losses.

"Michael and Bricey didn't dream it would come to their

death. They didn't," Fridfinnson told *CBC News*. "Bricey said the

exact same thing that Michael said [before he died]. 'I didn't want to grow up to be like this.'"[4]

PERSONAL AND SOCIAL FALLOUT

Fridfinnson's story is tragic. But what happened to her family is certainly not unique. For many family members and friends of

ADDICTION FACTORS

Some people who try cocaine once become immediately addicted. Others can use it many times without getting hooked. Many factors determine a person's response to the drug and risk for addiction.

- Age: The younger a person is when drug use starts, the more likely he or she will become addicted. Approximately 90 percent of people with drug addictions began smoking, drinking, or doing drugs before they turned 18.[5]

- Family and social dynamics: Peer pressure, stress, abuse, and lack of confidence can push a vulnerable person to start—and keep—using.

- Genes: Some addictive tendencies are passed down between family members, from generation to generation.

- Mental health: Mental illness and control-oriented behaviors, such as eating disorders, cutting, and other forms of acting out, can increase the likelihood of drug addiction.

people addicted to cocaine and other drugs, dealing with a drug user's erratic behavior can be frustrating and disheartening. It can also be difficult to figure out the difference between a one-time experiment with drugs and a problem that has morphed into a full-blown addiction.

As with many situations involving drugs, addiction starts small. There are plenty of telltale signs. First, normal behavioral patterns shift. Cocaine and crack addicts need the drug to feel normal, alert, and confident, so they will do anything to get their hands on a supply. Grades drop. Interest in extracurricular activities and hobbies dries up. Lateness or absence from a job becomes a regular occurrence. For teens like Michael, a change in friend groups or romantic partners—from responsible to

When a person becomes addicted to cocaine or any other drugs, it can disrupt relationships with family members and friends.

irresponsible, or from non-drug users to heavy drug users—is common.

As the habit progresses, many people who are addicted to cocaine take dangerous risks to get their next high. Some start selling drugs or stealing money in order to pay for a stash. Others move out and live on the street in order to snort coke or smoke crack in peace and without fear of judgment. Still others

have sex with strangers or their dealers in order to get the drug. Sometimes the situation becomes so dire that parents and friends refuse support, stage an intervention, or give up altogether.

While a cocaine user might feel on top of the world, one of the most important things they don't have is time. Once people start using cocaine or crack frequently, they will experience withdrawal if they don't get access to the drug on a regular basis. The process isn't pretty to watch or to endure.

COCAINE AND WEIGHT LOSS

Despite its obvious risks, many users insist that a benefit of doing cocaine is that they lose weight—even if all they eat is unhealthful foods like potato chips and pizza. In most cases, the claim is true. Cocaine suppresses the body's natural ability to desire food. But there is a reason for that, and it is not healthy. A study published in the scientific journal *Appetite* shows that cocaine actually prevents the body from storing fat.[7] As soon as a user stops doing the drug, the weight immediately returns. The weight is also harder to keep off because the body's metabolism has been so drastically altered.

WITHSTANDING WITHDRAWAL

Weaning oneself off any substance, especially a hard drug like cocaine, is no easy matter. Withdrawal symptoms can range from the temporary to the downright agonizing. The physical side effects are the most noticeable.

When coming down from cocaine, it takes about 90 minutes for the body to react.[6] Users often complain of feeling tired or distracted. They get increasingly anxious, and physical discomfort sets in. Depending on the length of the addiction and how much cocaine the user did on a regular basis, a range of other symptoms begin to take over. A person in withdrawal may experience muscle aches, nerve pain, chills, and involuntary shaking of the arms, legs, hands, and feet.

In addition to the physical side effects, people going through withdrawal also may experience a deterioration of their mental and emotional faculties. Users can become restless, confused, irrational, and even violent. Sometimes they commit heinous crimes, including abusive behavior, robbery, or even physical assault. In the most drastic cases— especially involving people who have no psychological support— the response to withdrawal can turn deadly. Some cocaine users who can't find their fix quickly enough contemplate or commit suicide.

THE THREAT OF SUICIDE

Even for someone without a prior history of mental illness, coming off of cocaine can cause nightmares. Withdrawal can also spark deep depression, paranoia, and an uncontrollable urge to get back on the drug by whatever means necessary. The mental effects of mixing cocaine and alcohol can be particularly dangerous— especially for people who have dealt with psychological issues in the past. According to a 2016 study published by Brown University and funded by the National Institutes of Mental Health, people who abused both alcohol and cocaine were 2.4 times more likely to kill themselves than other people with suicidal tendencies or other severe emotional disturbances.[8]

In any situation involving a serious cocaine or crack addiction, it is vitally important for the person suffering from withdrawal to get help. Sometimes an intervention from family and friends is enough to break the cycle. But in more severe cases, professional medical attention is a must. From 24-hour hotlines to hospitals to rehabilitation and drug treatment centers, there is a range of local and national options to choose from. The worst thing a cocaine user can do is nothing at all.

CHAPTER EIGHT

GETTING HELP

According to the Substance Abuse and Mental Health Services Administration's National Survey on Drug Use and Health, approximately 21 million people in the United States age 12 or older needed substance use treatment in 2016.[1] What that means is about 7.8 percent of people age 12 and older, or 1 in 13 people, needed professional help for drug addiction.[2] That same year, only 3.8 million people age 12 or older actually received the substance use treatment they required to get better.[3]

Those numbers are disheartening. As people like Demi Lovato and Lois Fridfinnson know, conquering a cocaine addiction is no easy matter. But getting the necessary treatment is crucial to becoming healthy again.

National help hotlines, regular appointments

People who are addicted to cocaine may feel isolated and hopeless, but with help from treatment centers, they can recover.

with mental health professionals, and drug rehabilitation programs are all methods that have been proven effective. Kicking a persistent drug habit is nearly impossible to do without the proper care and guidance.

Put simply, drug addiction is a brain disease, not a moral failing. It changes the way the brain works. People who use cocaine want the drug all the time, even if they know it's not good for them. They need to be taught how to function without it. Treatment can help chip away at the problem. During the recovery process, it is best if addicts are watched closely by doctors or mental health professionals in case something goes wrong.

In 2016, 1.1 million teens age 12 to 17 needed treatment for problems with substance use. Only 180,000 of them actually got the help they needed.[4]

INPATIENT REHAB CENTERS

No single type of treatment is right for everyone. People who are addicted to cocaine and think they need help getting sober have many options. For some of the most serious or long-term cases, an inpatient plan is often the best option. In these types of drug rehab programs, patients live in a facility with other drug users and are supervised by trained personnel and doctors. Patients are encouraged to stay until they feel strong enough to go back into the world and survive on their own without cocaine.

At inpatient rehab, patients are often required to attend lectures or health classes. They can also participate in group and one-on-one therapy sessions with professional counselors. Some programs last as little as a few weeks. Others can go on for six months to a year or more. Nearly all of these rehab facilities charge patients money, and the total fee can be substantial depending on the length of the stay.

Though some people with addictions report feeling trapped during rehab, and the experience isn't right for everyone, inpatient centers have many benefits. Doctors and nurses are available day and night to help drug abusers through the withdrawal process. They can provide psychiatric counseling and emotional support. In some cases, the staff is allowed to give patients medication to manage withdrawal symptoms and prevent relapses. It is also not uncommon for patients at these facilities to form a tight-knit

QUESTIONS TO ASK BEFORE TREATMENT

Admitting to cocaine abuse is a big first step. But finding the right form of treatment, and figuring out how to pay for it, can be confusing and scary. When talking to a drug counselor or calling a drug treatment hotline, here are some important questions to ask:

- What types of therapy work best?
- What happens in rehab?
- What does detoxing feel like?
- Are there medications for cocaine addiction?
- Where is the closest recovery center?
- What are the financial aid options for treatment?

community of people in various stages of recovery who are all going through withdrawal. Many report that it's comforting to be surrounded by others facing similar life challenges.

Halfway housing is another part of many inpatient rehab center programs. After patients are done with treatment, the halfway houses serve as a first step back into the world. Many of these sober apartments or houses are staffed with drug-free supervisors. These social workers or other trained professionals help recovering addicts search for jobs or apply to college, take control of their finances, and find positive role models they can depend on.

OUTPATIENT THERAPY

If inpatient care isn't an option, outpatient therapies have also proven to be successful. Most are a combination of behavioral and cognitive therapies that teach people with cocaine addictions how to modify their thinking and actions surrounding drug use. Recovering addicts can talk through their thoughts, emotions,

WILDERNESS RECOVERY PROGRAMS

Wilderness recovery programs are an alternative to inpatient rehab centers. Trained mental health and substance abuse counselors take people on month-long or multi-month excursions in the woods. Recovering addicts use this time to take their minds off their cocaine cravings and learn new pathways to healthy living. Participants sleep in tents, cook their own food, and take part in a slew of activities, including hiking, rock climbing, and survival training.

and drug cravings, and they can learn how to handle each in a mindful and responsible way. Patients usually meet with a certified therapist or counselor multiple times in the first few weeks after quitting cocaine. During this time, recovering addicts are the most vulnerable to triggers, and the tendency to relapse is the strongest.

Group therapy can be an important step in recovering from cocaine addiction.

CHALLENGES TO RECOVERY

Recovering fully from cocaine addiction means overcoming many obstacles. Some of the biggest roadblocks include:

- Admitting the cocaine abuse is a problem
- Finding enough money to pay for treatment for as long as treatment is needed
- Getting enough emotional support from family members, friends, and romantic partners to last through the entire treatment process
- Feeling self-confident enough to understand that all people deserve treatment, no matter what the circumstances might be
- Making and sticking with lifestyle changes so that future cocaine use is not an option
- Steering clear of people and situations that may spark the urge to do cocaine, including drug-using friends or abusive romantic partners

Teenagers dealing with drug addiction can go to family therapy with their parents, guardians, or siblings. This provides a chance for everyone to be honest, air their complaints, and learn how to be supportive during the treatment process. It is critical that teens still be treated individually as well, either by an experienced drug counselor at school or by an independent psychiatrist. Young people need someone they can trust who can remain objective while also being on their side no matter what. Sometimes a family member is part of the initial problem.

In addition to traditional therapies, many recovering cocaine users get involved in alternative treatment methods that help take their mind off their cravings. Meditation helps people relax and advocates a

Alternative methods of relieving stress, such as yoga and meditation, can play an important role during the process of breaking a cocaine addiction.

mindful approach to living. Yoga and frequent exercise, including aerobics, running, or any team sport, get the body moving and feeling energized. These activities are natural substitutes for the unhealthy chemical high brought on by doing cocaine.

AFTER TREATMENT

Whether it's inpatient or outpatient therapy, the most important requirement for someone recovering from a cocaine addiction is ongoing support. Ideally, that means family and friends will try

their hardest to encourage and be a part of the healing process, even if a relapse occurs.

Sadly, for many cocaine abusers, especially habitual users, rehab is not a onetime event. According to the National Institute on Drug Abuse, between 40 and 60 percent of recovering addicts slip up and do drugs again.[5] Relapse is an all-too-common pitfall, but it is not an indication of failure or that treatment won't work in the future.

Relapse happens when a person who has tried to quit using cocaine starts doing the drug again. More often than not, a person starts up again because of an increase in stress levels or because they are triggered by a person or type of behavior that made them want to do the drug in the past. There are many reasons a person might relapse in response to a trigger. The most obvious example is being around cocaine at a party, getting a phone call from an old drug-using buddy, or running into a dealer on the street. Triggers can also be subtler, such as a specific smell, a weather pattern, or music by a particular band or singer.

Luckily, there are still more resources available to help prevent relapses from happening. Many towns across the United States, through religious or community organizations, run weekly or monthly support meetings where people with drug problems can go to get help. National groups, such as Cocaine Anonymous,

Narcotics Anonymous (NA), and Drug Abuse Resistance Education (D.A.R.E.), have chapters throughout the United States and the world. For people who feel uncomfortable sharing their private thoughts and feelings in a group or who need help right away, there are a number of 24-hour hotlines to call that are free of charge.

Cocaine addiction can happen to anyone. People suffering from drug problems come in all shapes and sizes and are of every gender, race, and age. But just because the problem is so common doesn't mean it is unsolvable or irreversible. With the proper treatment—and plenty of love and support—it is possible to leave cocaine or crack behind and never touch the drug again. Despite how improbable it might seem, a chance at sobriety is never too far out of reach.

DRUG TREATMENT HOTLINES

Drug treatment hotlines exist to empower drug users to take the next step toward getting well. They are staffed by trained drug counselors, free to use, and available at any hour of the day or night. Some, such as the National Cocaine Hotline (1-800-COCAINE), are crisis hotlines. Others, like the National Drug Information Treatment and Referral Hotline (800-662-HELP), provide information and treatment referrals.

ESSENTIAL FACTS

EFFECTS ON THE BODY

- On the surface, cocaine appears to help users feel awake, confident, outgoing, and mentally sharp. But upon closer investigation, clear signs reveal that the drug is both dangerous and deadly.

- Whether it's snorted, injected, or smoked, cocaine or crack has disastrous effects on the brain and other organs. In mild cases, users can become irritable, irrational, and aggressive. More serious side effects include kidney failure, bleeding in the brain, seizures, heart attack, and stroke. Withdrawal symptoms, such as uncontrollable shakes, nightmares, and suicidal thoughts, are brutal to endure.

- Cocaine addiction can affect people of any age, race, gender, and cultural background. It is possible to die from cocaine even on the first try.

LAWS AND POLICIES

- In the United States, a number of laws and policies have shaped the way cocaine and other drugs—and their users—are treated. The first major drug law on the books was the Harrison Narcotics Tax Act of 1914. It put a tax on all people who manufactured or sold coca leaves or cocaine in any form.

- In 1970, President Richard Nixon signed the Controlled Substances Act into law, which set up rules for regulating the manufacture, trafficking, possession, sale, and use of controlled substances, such as hallucinogens, narcotics, depressants, and stimulants. It also divided these drugs into separate categories called schedules, according to their level of addictiveness.

- The Anti–Drug Abuse Act was passed in 1986. It set up mandatory prison sentences for drug offenses, like carrying cocaine and crack. This law disproportionately affected lower-class African Americans in a negative way.

IMPACT ON SOCIETY

- According to the 2017 World Drug Report, in 2016, nearly 1,200 short tons (1,090 metric tons) of 100 percent pure cocaine was manufactured in countries such as Colombia, Peru, and Bolivia and illegally trafficked to the United States and countries around the world.

- In 2016, approximately 28,000 teens (age 12 to 17) used cocaine and 3,000 used crack. Nearly 552,000 young adults (age 18 to 25) used cocaine and 15,000 used crack.

- The manufacturing and sale of cocaine has become a worldwide epidemic. It has created crime waves in cities and rural areas and overcrowding in jails. Millions of taxpayer dollars are spent to help people with drug addictions get clean.

QUOTE

"When you're an addict, nothing can get through to you. I never thought I was going to die. I never thought I'd be in a coma. I didn't think I had a problem. But then I woke up in a bed with tubes coming out of my mouth—and it was real."

—Retired NBA player Lamar Odom

GLOSSARY

ABSTINENCE
The practice of not doing or having something that is desired, such as drinking alcohol.

ANESTHESIA
A drug given to a person to cause loss of consciousness and block pain, such as in surgery.

COGNITIVE
Related to the act or process of thinking, reasoning, remembering, imagining, or learning.

DILUTE
To make a substance weaker by adding other elements to it.

ERADICATION
The complete removal or destruction of something.

ERRATIC
Unpredictable or unusual.

EUPHORIC
Characterized by an intense feeling of happiness or bliss.

FATIGUE
Extreme tiredness.

INSOMNIA
The inability to fall asleep and stay asleep.

INTRAVENOUS
Happening within or entering through a vein.

NARCOTIC
A drug that affects a person's brain and is often dangerous and against the law to have, sell, or use.

NEUROLOGIST
A doctor who treats disorders that affect the brain, spinal cord, and nerves.

NEUROSES
Mental illness; types of strange or anxious thoughts or worries.

OPHTHALMOLOGIST
A doctor who specializes in vision and eye care.

RELAPSE
To fall or slip back into a former practice.

SOBRIETY
The state of being sober; not under the influence of alcohol or mind-altering drugs.

STIMULANT
A category of drug that affects the nervous system and increases the body's heart rate and blood pressure.

ADDITIONAL RESOURCES

SELECTED BIBLIOGRAPHY

"Cocaine." *Research Reports*. National Institute on Drug Abuse, May 2016. Web. 15 Nov. 2017.

"Demi Lovato: Simply Complicated." *YouTube*. Google, 17 Oct. 2017. Web. 15 Nov. 2017.

Johnston, Lloyd D., Patrick M. O'Malley, Richard A. Meich, Jerald G. Bachman, and John E. Schulenberg. "Cocaine" and "Crack." Monitoring the Future: National Survey on Drug Use (2016 Overview: Key Findings on Adolescent Drug Use), 2017, 19–22.

UNODC Research. "World Drug Report 2017." *UNODC.org*. United Nations Office on Drugs and Crime, 16 June 2017. Web. 15 Nov. 2017.

FURTHER READINGS

Bodden, Valerie. *Club and Prescription Drug Abuse*. Minneapolis: Abdo, 2015. Print.

Shantz-Hilkes, Chloe. *Hooked: When Addiction Hits Home*. Toronto, Canada: Annick, 2013. Print.

ONLINE RESOURCES

Booklinks
NONFICTION NETWORK
FREE! ONLINE NONFICTION RESOURCES

To learn more about cocaine, visit **abdobooklinks.com.** These links are routinely monitored and updated to provide the most current information available.

MORE INFORMATION

For more information on this subject, contact or visit the following organizations:

DRUG FREE AMERICA FOUNDATION
5999 Central Avenue, Suite 301
Saint Petersburg, FL 33710
727-828-0211
dfaf.org

The bold mission of this drug prevention and policy organization is to develop and promote national and international policies and laws that will help stop illegal drug use and drug addiction. The group includes Students Taking Action Not Drugs (STAND), a division dedicated to distributing information on drugs and addiction to students nationwide.

NATIONAL INSTITUTE ON DRUG ABUSE FOR TEENS (NIDA)
9000 Rockville Pike
Bethesda, MD 20892
301-496-4000
teens.drugabuse.gov

This site is part of the National Institute on Drug Abuse (NIDA), National Institutes of Health (NIH), and the US Department of Health and Human Services (HHS). It contains all sorts of useful information about drugs, their effects, addiction, and how to get help.

SOURCE NOTES

CHAPTER 1. A BATTLE WITH COCAINE ADDICTION

1. *Demi Lovato: Simply Complicated.* YouTube. 17 Oct. 2017. Web. 15 Nov. 2017.
2. Alyssa Toomey. "Demi Lovato Talks Past Drug Use: 'I Couldn't Go 30 Minutes to an Hour without Cocaine.'" *E! News.* E! Entertainment Television, 10 Dec. 2013. Web. 15 Nov. 2017.
3. *Demi Lovato: Simply Complicated.*
4. *Demi Lovato: Simply Complicated.*
5. *Demi Lovato: Simply Complicated.*
6. *Demi Lovato: Simply Complicated.*
7. *Demi Lovato: Simply Complicated.*
8. Christopher Woody. "Cocaine Prices in the US Have Barely Moved in Decades— Here's How Cartels Distort the Market." *Business Insider.* Business Insider, 13 Oct. 2016. Web. 15 Nov. 2017.

CHAPTER 2. WHAT IS COCAINE?

1. Eunice Park-Lee, et al. "Receipt of Services for Substance Use and Mental Health Issues among Adults: Results from the 2016 National Survey on Drug Use and Health." *Substance Abuse and Mental Health Services Administration.* SAMHSA, Sept. 2017. Web. 5 Jan. 2018.
2. Phillip Smith. "The World's Highest (and Lowest) Cocaine Prices." *AlterNet.* Independent Media Institute, 10 June 2015. Web. 15 Nov. 2017.
3. "What You Need to Know about Freebasing Cocaine." *American Addiction Centers.* American Addiction Centers, n.d. Web. 15 Nov. 2017.
4. "Drug Facts: What Is Cocaine?" *National Institute on Drug Abuse.* National Institute on Drug Abuse, June 2016. Web. 15 Nov. 2017.
5. "How Long Does Cocaine Stay in Your System?" *American Addiction Centers.* American Addiction Centers, n.d. Web. 15 Nov. 2017.
6. "Retail Cocaine Prices." *Narcotic News.* Narcotic News, 2017. Web. 15 Nov. 2017.
7. "Cocaine and Crack Facts." *Drug Policy Alliance.* Drug Policy Alliance, n.d. Web. 15 Nov. 2017.
8. "Kicking the Habit: The Drug Addicts Who Nearly Lost It All." *BBC News.* BBC News Services, 29 Oct. 2017. Web. 15 Nov. 2017.
9. "Kicking the Habit: The Drug Addicts Who Nearly Lost It All."
10. "Kicking the Habit: The Drug Addicts Who Nearly Lost It All."
11. Lloyd D. Johnston, et al. "2016 Overview: Key Findings on Adolescent Drug Use." *National Institute on Drug Abuse.* NIDA, 2017. Web. 19–22. 13 Apr. 2018.

CHAPTER 3. COCAINE'S ORIGINS

1. Donald Cains, ed. *Essentials of Pharmaceutical Chemistry*. London, UK: Pharmaceutical Press, 2012. Print. 267.

2. Tom Blickman. "Coca Leaf: Myths and Reality." *Transnational Institute*. TNI, 5 Aug. 2014. Web. 15 Nov. 2017.

3. Justin Clemens. *Psychoanalysis Is an Antiphilosophy*. Edinburgh, Scotland: Edinburgh UP, 2013. Print. 28.

4. Christopher Woody. "Coca Production Is Booming in Colombia—Here's How It Gets Turned into Cocaine." *Business Insider*. Business Insider, 18 Oct. 2017. Web. 15 Nov. 2017.

5. Jeremy Lesser. "Today Is the 100th Anniversary of the Harrison Narcotics Tax Act." *Drug Policy Alliance*. Drug Policy Alliance, 16 Dec. 2014. Web. 15 Nov. 2017.

CHAPTER 4. COCAINE AND THE LAW

1. "Cocaine Cassie: The Prison Interview." *60 Minutes Australia*. CBS News Productions, 24 Sept. 2017. Web. 12 Apr. 2018.

2. "Cocaine Cassie: The Prison Interview."

3. "Cocaine Cassie: The Prison Interview."

4. "Cocaine Cassie: The Prison Interview."

5. "Cocaine Cassie: The Prison Interview."

6. "Cocaine Cassie: The Prison Interview."

7. Nick Miroff. "American Cocaine Use Is Way Up. Colombia's Coca Boom Might Be Why." *Washington Post*. Nash Holdings LLC, 4 Mar. 2017. Web. 15 Nov. 2017.

8. "Quick Facts: Drug Trafficking Offenses." *United States Sentencing Commission*. USSC, n.d. Web. 15 Nov. 2017.

9. Miroff, "American Cocaine Use Is Way Up."

10. Miroff, "American Cocaine Use Is Way Up."

11. Miroff, "American Cocaine Use Is Way Up."

12. Miroff, "American Cocaine Use Is Way Up."

13. Miroff, "American Cocaine Use Is Way Up."

14. "Drug Scheduling." *United States Drug Enforcement Administration*. DEA, n.d. Web. 15 Nov. 2017.

15. "Drugs of Abuse: A DEA Resource Guide." *United States Drug Enforcement Administration*. DEA, 2017. Web. 18 Jan. 2018.

16. "Oregon Board of Pharmacy Laws & Rules." *State of Oregon*. State of Oregon, Jan. 2018. Web. 15 Jan. 2018.

17. "Oregon Board of Pharmacy Laws & Rules."

18. Danielle Kurtzleben. "Data Show Racial Disparity in Crack Sentencing." *US News & World Report*. US News & World Report, 3 Aug. 2010. Web. 15 Nov. 2017.

SOURCE NOTES CONTINUED

CHAPTER 5. COCAINE AND THE BRAIN

1. "Drug Facts: Cocaine and Your Brain." *Heads Up*. Scholastic, 2003. Web. 15 Nov. 2017.
2. "Drug Facts: Cocaine and Your Brain."
3. Alexander W. Morton. "Cocaine and Psychiatric Symptoms." *Primary Care Companion to the Journal of Clinical Psychiatry*. National Center for Biotechnology Information, Aug. 1999. Web. 15 Nov. 2017.

CHAPTER 6. COCAINE AND THE BODY

1. Mark Shrayber. "Is Your Casual Cocaine Use Dangerous?" *Uproxx*. Uproxx, 6 Nov. 2016. Web. 15 Nov. 2017.
2. "Bolger—Message to Cocaine Users." *American Heart Association*. American Heart Association, n.d. Web. 15 Nov. 2017.
3. Adam Lusher. "The Flesh-Eating, Bladder-Wrecking Chemicals Hidden in Street Cocaine." *Independent*. Independent, 14 Sept. 2016. Web. 15 Nov. 2017.
4. Lusher, "The Flesh-Eating, Bladder-Wrecking Chemicals Hidden in Street Cocaine."
5. "Here's What Your Eyes Look Like When You Take Different Drugs." *Vice*. Vice Media, 14 Nov. 2014. Web. 15 Nov. 2017.
6. "Drug Facts: Cocaine and Your Brain." *Heads Up*. Scholastic, 2003. Web. 15 Nov. 2017.
7. "What Are the Effects of Maternal Cocaine Use?" *Drugs, Brains, and Behavior: The Science of Addiction*. National Institute on Drug Abuse, May 2016. Web. 15 Nov. 2017.
8. "Overdose Death Rates." *Drugs, Brains, and Behavior: The Science of Addiction*. National Institute on Drug Abuse, Sept. 2017. Web. 15 Nov. 2017.
9. Lamar Odom. "Done in the Dark." *Players' Tribune*. Players' Tribune, 27 Jul. 2017. Web. 15 Nov. 2017.
10. Alexia Fernandez. "Lamar Odom 'Is Spiraling Again' Following His Collapse, Says Source." *People*. Time, 6 Nov. 2017. Web. 15 Nov. 2017.

CHAPTER 7. CONSEQUENCES OF ADDICTION

1. Janice Grant. "'I Can't Be Losing Another Child': Mom Who Lost 2 Kids to Drugs Wants Longer-Term Services for Addicts." *CBC News*. CBC/Radio-Canada, 14 Jun. 2017. Web. 15 Nov. 2017.

2. Grant, "'I Can't Be Losing Another Child.'"

3. Grant, "'I Can't Be Losing Another Child.'"

4. Grant, "'I Can't Be Losing Another Child.'"

5. "Addiction by the Numbers." *National Center on Addiction and Substance Abuse*. NCASA, n.d. Web. 15 Nov. 2017.

6. "Cocaine Withdrawal Symptoms, Timeline, and Treatment." *American Addiction Centers*. American Addiction Centers, n.d. Web. 15 Nov. 2017.

7. "Cocaine Doesn't Just Curb Appetite, It Suppresses the Body's Ability to Store Fat Too, Find Scientists." *DailyMail.com*. Associated Newspapers, 9 Aug. 2013. Web. 15 Nov. 2017.

8. David Orenstein. "Simultaneous Cocaine, Alcohol Use Linked to Suicide Risk." *New from Brown*. Brown University, 8 Apr. 2016. Web. 15 Nov. 2017.

CHAPTER 8. GETTING HELP

1. "Key Substance Use and Mental Health Indicators in the United States: Results from the 2016 National Survey on Drug Use and Health." *Substance Abuse and Mental Health Services Administration*. SAMHSA, 2017. Web. 15 Nov. 2017.

2. "Key Substance Use and Mental Health Indicators in the United States."

3. "Key Substance Use and Mental Health Indicators in the United States."

4. "Key Substance Use and Mental Health Indicators in the United States."

5. "Drugs, Brains, and Behavior: The Science of Addiction." *National Institute on Drug Abuse*. NIDA, n.d. Web. 15 Nov. 2017.

INDEX

ABOUT THE AUTHOR

Alexis Burling has written dozens of articles and books for young readers on a variety of topics including current events and famous people, nutrition and fitness, careers and money management, relationships, and cooking. She is also a book critic, with reviews of both adult and young adult books, author interviews, and other industry-related articles published in the *New York Times*, the *Washington Post*, the *San Francisco Chronicle*, and more. Burling lives in Portland, Oregon, with her husband.